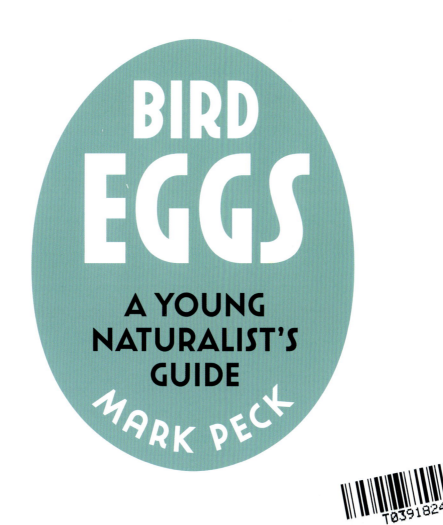

# BIRD EGGS

## A YOUNG NATURALIST'S GUIDE

### MARK PECK

FIREFLY BOOKS

# A Firefly Book

Published by Firefly Books Ltd. 2024
Copyright © 2024 Firefly Books Ltd.
Text copyright © 2024 Mark Peck

Photographs © 2024 Mark Peck, except as listed on page 80.

All rights reserved. No part of this publication may be reproduced, stored in a retrieval system, or transmitted in any form or by any means, electronic, mechanical, photocopying, recording or otherwise, without the prior written permission of the Publisher.

First printing

Library of Congress Control Number: 2024932960

Library and Archives Canada Cataloguing in Publication
Title: Bird eggs : a young naturalist's guide / Mark Peck.
Names: Peck, Mark K. (Mark Kelday), 1959– author.
Description: Includes index.
Identifiers: Canadiana 20240326555 | ISBN 9780228104834 (hardcover) | ISBN 9780228104827 (softcover)
Subjects: LCSH: Birds—Eggs—Juvenile literature.
LCGFT: Informational works.
Classification: LCC QL675 .P45 2024 | DDC j598.14/68—dc23

Published in the United States by
Firefly Books (U.S.) Inc.
P.O. Box 1338, Ellicott Station
Buffalo, New York 14205

Published in Canada by
Firefly Books Ltd.
50 Staples Avenue, Unit 1
Richmond Hill, Ontario L4B 0A7

Cover and interior design: Gareth Lind, Lind Design
Printed in China | E

We acknowledge the financial support of the Government of Canada.

# CONTENTS

**INTRODUCTION: WHAT CAME FIRST, THE CHICKEN OR THE EGG? 5**

**CHAPTER 1: ALL ABOUT EGGS 6**
What Is an Egg? 6
How Are Eggs Made? 7
Who Lays Eggs? 9
How Many Eggs? 10
Timing and Incubation 16
Brood Parasitism 24
Egg Predators 28

**CHAPTER 2: SIZE 34**

**CHAPTER 3: SHAPE 40**

**CHAPTER 4: COLOR 45**

**CHAPTER 5: LOCATION 58**
Tree Nesting 58
Cavity Nesting 62
Ground Nesting 64
Underground Nesting 66
Nesting on Water 68
Nesting on Human-made Structures 70

**CHAPTER 6: CONSERVATION AND PROTECTION 74**
Monitoring Nests 74
Getting Involved 76
Building Nest Boxes 77

Glossary 78
Index 79
Acknowledgments 80
Photo Credits 80

A female Ostrich guards her nest full of eggs.

## INTRODUCTION

# WHAT CAME FIRST, THE CHICKEN OR THE EGG?

Although this question has been asked for thousands of years, the answer is easy. Eggs have been around for a *very* long time. In fact, eggs were around long before there were birds, let alone chickens. Many **invertebrate\*** and **vertebrate** animals lay eggs, and that has been true for hundreds of millions of years — before the animals we see today even existed. As you may know, dinosaurs laid eggs. Eggs have evolved in different ways in many different animal groups. They are a key part of **reproduction** and have played a crucial role in the success of so many animals living today.

Bird eggs in particular are beautiful and mysterious, and we can learn so much from them. The study of bird eggs is known as oology. Its focus is the collection, preservation and research of bird eggs. More than 100 years ago, oology was a very popular study and hobby. It provided valuable information on bird biology, breeding behavior and **ecology**. However, collecting bird eggs was not good for wild birds or their survival. Thankfully, egg collecting is now illegal in most countries. These collections still exist, but now you can only find them in museums and other research institutions. Researchers still study bird eggs and use historical collections, but they don't need to collect any more eggs.

Studying and monitoring eggs, nests and breeding birds is more important than ever, especially in a world that's changing so quickly. Climate change, habitat loss and **predators** are dangerous threats to bird populations around the world.

By understanding how breeding birds are affected by these threats, we can find solutions to help birds as well as protect the natural world we all live in. We can answer questions like:

- **Are birds nesting earlier in the year due to changes in our climate?**
- **Are species nesting in different habitats, and are they adapting to human-made changes to their habitats?**
- **What impacts are predators having on nesting birds?**
- **Are birds successfully raising their young each year?**

There are so many questions to be answered, but it all begins with an appreciation for the natural world around us. I hope this book inspires you to get outside, keep your eyes open and take in the wonders of nature, both big and small. I also hope it encourages you to help find solutions to many of the problems birds are facing today and in the future.

**\*All terms in bold are defined in the glossary on page 78.**

# CHAPTER 1
# ALL ABOUT EGGS

## WHAT IS AN EGG?

When you think of an egg, you probably think of a chicken egg. But did you know that almost all animals start out as an egg? That's right, birds, reptiles, fish, insects and mammals all come from an egg. Even you, a human, began as an egg. An egg is the structure many animals use to produce their young. Eggs are amazing. Each one begins as a single cell and eventually grows into something as complex as a bird, an alligator or a person.

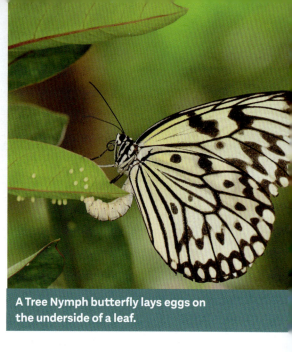
A Tree Nymph butterfly lays eggs on the underside of a leaf.

**There are three types of egg-producing animals:**

Virginia Rail

### Oviparous
Most fish, reptiles, amphibians, insects and all birds lay their eggs outside of their bodies.

Whale Shark

### Ovoviviparous
Some sharks, snakes and lizards keep their eggs inside their bodies until they hatch.

Chimpanzee

### Viviparous
Finally, most mammals and some fish, including seahorses, receive nutrients and oxygen directly from their parent as they grow.

## HOW ARE EGGS MADE?

An egg starts out as a tiny cell produced by a female animal. Female birds have many egg cells (called ova) when they are born. As the bird gets older some of the cells will begin to grow during the breeding season. When the time is right, one of the egg cells is released into the **ovary** and grows into a yolk. The yolk contains all the nutrients needed for the **embryo** to grow and develop properly.

Once the yolk is fully formed it starts traveling down the oviduct, where it is **fertilized**. The oviduct looks like a long, flexible, rubbery tube. Once inside the oviduct, the egg white (albumen) is added around the yolk. The albumen is important because it helps protect the yolk and the growing embryo.

Next, two thin layers (called membranes) are added around the yolk and the egg white to keep everything together. There is also a small airspace between the two layers at the bigger end of the egg that will continue to enlarge as the embryo develops. This space also helps oxygen and carbon dioxide move in and out of the egg. Finally, the eggshell is added over several hours.

For animals that lay their eggs outside of their bodies, the eggshell is very important.

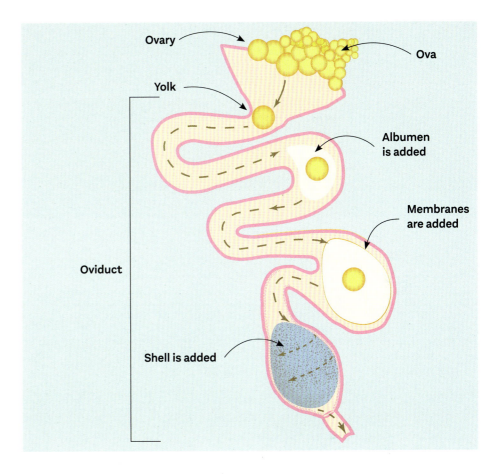

It is strong and helps protect the growing embryo from injury and disease. The eggshell is also **porous** and allows in just the right amount of water, oxygen and carbon dioxide for a safe and stable environment inside. Bird eggshells are made of a material called calcium carbonate — the same stuff that shells, chalk and pearls are made of. Birds get calcium from the food they eat. Female birds store extra calcium in their bones before they start laying their eggs.

Colored **pigments** may also be added as the eggshell is being made. Although bird eggs come in a beautiful variety of colors and patterns, there are only two pigments responsible for the whole range of colors. You may notice some eggshells have streaks and/or spots. An egg will be spotted if it is still when the colors are added. It will have streaks if the egg is moving.

At this point the egg is ready to be laid. The whole process takes about 24 hours to complete, but it can be longer for bigger birds and bigger eggs.

7

**You'll need:**
- A fresh, uncooked egg
- A drinking glass
- White vinegar
- Foil or plastic wrap

# Dissolving an Eggshell

**Want to see what an egg looks like without its shell? Try this fun experiment to dissolve an egg's calcium carbonate shell and reveal the membrane underneath!**

## DAY 1
Gently place the egg in the drinking glass and pour over the vinegar until it completely covers the egg. You will notice the surface of the egg will start to form bubbles. This means the acidic vinegar is starting to dissolve the egg's calcium carbonate shell. Cover the glass with foil or plastic wrap and place it in the fridge for a day.

## DAY 2
The next day, drain the vinegar (taking care not to let the egg roll out of the glass). Observe how the egg looks. Is there still some shell on it? It takes at least two days to fully dissolve the eggshell, so fill the glass with some new vinegar, cover it and store it in the fridge for another day.

## DAY 3
By the third day, the eggshell should be completely gone. Drain the vinegar and gently pat the egg dry. Observe how the egg feels in your hand. You can even test how strong the egg's membrane is by doing drop tests outside or in your kitchen sink. Start close to the ground and then gradually increase the height. How high can you drop it before the membrane breaks?

## WHO LAYS EGGS?

There are close to 11,000 different species of birds in the world, and they all lay eggs. But only female birds make eggs. (Males help by fertilizing the egg.) Egg laying usually takes place in the spring and summer when the weather is warmer and there is plenty of food available. Food is important for both the growing chicks and the female, who needs lots of extra food and energy to make the eggs.

A female Pileated Woodpecker with her three hungry chicks.

## HOW MANY EGGS?

Clutch size is the number of eggs laid by a female bird during a single nesting attempt. The aim is to try to have as many chicks survive as possible. The number of eggs laid is different between species and sometimes even within a species.

There are several reasons why clutch size varies:

- **Availability of food (for both the adults and the young),**
- **The amount of care needed by the young,**
- **The type of nest,**
- **Where the nest is located,**
- **The time of year,**
- **The age and health of the female,**
- **Whether the bird breeds in a nesting colony and**
- **The risk of predators finding the eggs.**

Atlantic Puffins nest in burrows in colonies with other puffins. The female lays only one white egg. Colony-nesting species often have fewer eggs than other birds.

Ducks, like this Northern Pintail, have big clutches and often lay 10 or more eggs in their nests. Other **waterfowl**, like geese and the much larger Tundra Swan, usually lay only five or six eggs.

This Mourning Dove lays only two white eggs in its nest at a time, but some doves may try nesting as many as six times in one year, sometimes starting as early as February.

Almost all **shorebirds** that breed in the Arctic, like this Whimbrel, lay four eggs. Shorebirds that breed near the equator often lay only two.

Most North American **songbirds**, like the American Crow or the Blue Jay, lay four to six eggs in their nests. This Song Sparrow also lays four to six eggs, but it may try to nest two or three times in a breeding season.

14

Surprisingly, some of North America's smallest songbirds, like the Black-capped Chickadee or this Golden-crowned Kinglet, may lay as many as seven to 10 eggs in their nests.

## TIMING AND INCUBATION

A bird egg needs to be kept warm and safe while the embryo inside grows and develops. This is known as incubation. The incubation period is the amount of time birds must sit on their eggs before they hatch. Which parent will sit on the eggs, and for how long, differs among species. Most birds lay one egg a day until they have their full clutch. Some birds will begin incubating after laying the first egg, but others won't start until the last one is laid. If a bird lays many eggs and then waits until the last one is laid before starting incubation, all the eggs will hatch at about the same time. This makes it easier for the parents to care and feed their young.

To help keep the eggs warm, some birds develop what's called a brood patch. This is an area of skin on the belly of the bird where there are no feathers. This patch lets the parent keep the eggs at a warm, constant temperature and gives the bird direct contact with the egg so they can feel any changes taking place as the embryo grows.

**An American Avocet turns its eggs, revealing its brood patch near its right leg.**

Bald Eagles sit on their eggs for 35 days. Both parents incubate, but the female does it more than the male. Nesting may begin in late winter, and incubation starts when the first egg is laid. Eagles often lay two or three eggs over four or five days. This means young will be different ages in the nest.

The female Sharp-tailed Grouse begins nesting in late spring and sits on her eggs for 22 days once the last one is laid. All the eggs hatch around the same time, and the young leave the nest within 24 hours. Males do not help with nesting or taking care of the young.

Red-necked Phalaropes have the opposite strategy. Only the male sits on the eggs. The female leaves the nest soon after she lays her eggs in early June. The male incubates the eggs for 19 days until they hatch, and he only leaves the nest for short periods to feed.

The Rock Pigeon may nest at any time of the year, and sometimes more than once a year. Their incubation period is 18 days, and both parents take turns sitting on the eggs. Females usually sit on them at night, while males incubate during the day.

Short-eared Owls nest all across Canada and the northern United States. Only the female sits on the eggs, and she begins when the first one is laid. Nesting begins in early spring, but exactly when depends on where the birds live. For instance, birds that live farther south breed earlier in the year. Incubation is for 28 to 30 days.

Like most other warbler species, American Redstarts incubate their eggs for 11 or 12 days, usually starting in early June. Only females sit on the eggs, beginning when the last one has been laid. During that time the male defends the nesting territory. He will then help feed the young when the eggs hatch.

# Incubation Times across the Bird World

Check out the chart below to see how long these familiar birds usually incubate their eggs. How long do you think you could last?

| Bird | Incubation Time |
| --- | --- |
| American Robin | 12 days |
| Black-capped Chickadee | 12 days |
| Ruby-throated Hummingbird | 12 days |
| Golden-crowned Kinglet | 14 days |
| Pileated Woodpecker | 16 days |
| Blue Jay | 17 days |
| Common Raven | 21 days |
| Common Loon | 27 days |
| Great Blue Heron | 27 days |
| American White Pelican | 30 days |
| Snowy Owl | 33 days |
| Bald Eagle | 35 days |
| Mute Swan | 36 days |
| Atlantic Puffin | 42 days |
| Common Ostrich | 44 days |
| Emperor Penguin | 64 days |
| North Island Brown Kiwi | 79 days |
| Snowy Albatross | 79 days |

An American Robin incubating its eggs.

A Snowy Albatross nesting on the Falkland Islands.

## BROOD PARASITISM

Almost all birds take care of their own eggs, but, believe it or not, some species leave the care of their eggs to other birds. These types of birds are known as brood parasites, and they are more common than you might think. Some waterfowl, cuckoos and cowbirds are well known to lay their eggs in other nests.

A bird might lay its eggs in another bird's nest because then it does not have to use lots of energy building nests, caring for young or avoiding nest predators. Brood parasites can also lay more eggs in a variety of different bird nests, which means they might produce more young throughout the breeding season.

Having a stranger's egg in your nest can be a disadvantage if you're the host species though. The host species must spend time looking after another bird's eggs and young. Many will accept the strange egg as one of their own. However, some host species recognize parasitic eggs and may remove them, build a completely new nest in a different area or sometimes build a new nest directly on top of the parasitic egg and the old nest.

This Brown-headed Cowbird chick (left) demands food from its host, a Song Sparrow (right).

Wood Ducks nest in tree **cavities** and nest boxes, which are boxes specifically made for birds to nest in. When there is a lot of competition for nesting sites, some Wood Ducks will lay their eggs in another duck's nest. And sometimes other ducks, like the Hooded Merganser, will lay their eggs in a Wood Duck's nest. This is known as egg dumping. Egg dumping is more common early in the nesting season, when some ducks may not have found a nesting site. It also occurs more in nest boxes than in natural nesting sites.

Many of the close to 150 different species of cuckoos are brood parasites. The Common Cuckoo, which is found in Europe, is famous for laying its eggs in other birds' nests. The Yellow-billed and Black-billed Cuckoos in North America are also brood parasites, but they do things a little differently. Both cuckoos will build their own nests, but they will sometimes also lay their blue eggs in other nests, especially if the other bird's eggs are also blue. The Black-billed Cuckoo's egg is the one on the left.

The Brown-headed Cowbird does not build a nest. Instead, the female finds the nest of another bird and lays her white, spotted eggs in it. Cowbirds have laid their eggs in the nests of over 220 bird species. Over 144 of those have successfully raised cowbird young. Many of the young do not survive, so the female cowbird may lay as many as 40 eggs in one season.

## EGG PREDATORS

Bird eggs are a good source of protein and an excellent source of vitamins and minerals. Not surprisingly, there are lots of predators looking to eat them. Mammals who like to eat eggs include coyotes, foxes, raccoons, skunks and weasels. There are other egg-eating mammals that might surprise you: cats, squirrels, chipmunks, rats and even mice. Reptiles that eat eggs include snakes, lizards and turtles. However, some of the most dangerous egg predators are other birds like jays, ravens, crows, magpies and gulls. Birds use different methods to protect their eggs from these predators.

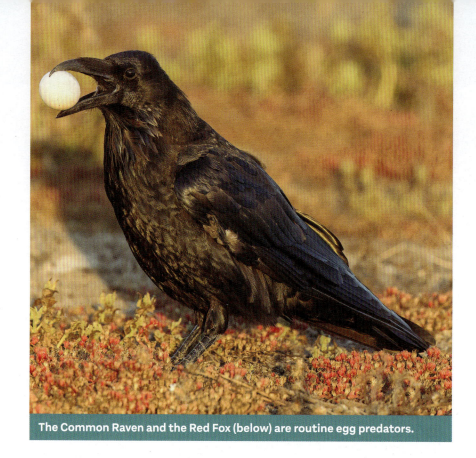

The Common Raven and the Red Fox (below) are routine egg predators.

Some birds conceal their nests well to protect their eggs. Ovenbirds build a grassy dome over their ground nest to help keep their eggs hidden from above.

29

Some birds nest in areas that are difficult for predators to access. Pileated Woodpeckers lay their eggs in tree cavities to protect them from both predators and the weather. Black-legged Kittiwakes (shown here) nest on steep cliffs, keeping their eggs safe from most predators.

Many birds, like this American Golden-Plover, remove the eggshells from the nest immediately after they hatch so predators are not attracted to the smell.

Other birds keep predators at bay by behaving in a certain way. Semipalmated Plovers will try to distract potential predators in order to lure them away from their eggs.

The Canada Goose can be very aggressive, scaring away potential egg predators (and even humans).

# CHAPTER 2
# SIZE

Bird eggs come in many sizes. The size depends on the differences in each species. In general, big birds lay big eggs and small birds lay small eggs, but it is more complicated than that. Some small birds lay very big eggs compared with their body size. Egg size is also related to the size of the chick. Some chicks are **altricial**, meaning they're born naked, blind and helpless and can develop in smaller eggs. Others are **precocial**, meaning they hatch more fully developed and active, covered in down and with their eyes open. These chicks need larger eggs to grow in.

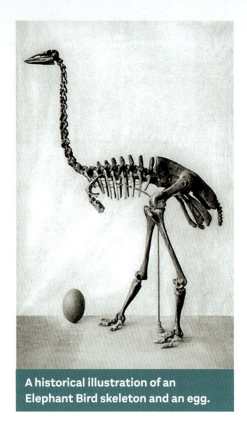

A historical illustration of an Elephant Bird skeleton and an egg.

① The largest bird egg belonged to the giant, flightless Elephant Bird. This bird was huge — it stood over 3 meters (9.8 feet) tall and may have weighed as much as 500 kilograms (1,120 pounds). Their eggs were huge too. One egg was equal to about 10 ostrich eggs and was about 35 centimeters (14 inches) long. The eggshell was also very thick so the egg would not be crushed when its colossal parent was sitting on it. Elephant Birds were found only on the island of Madagascar and went extinct about 1,000 years ago.

② The Common Ostrich lays the biggest egg in the world today. One ostrich egg is equal to about 20 chicken eggs. Ostrich eggs are big, but they are small compared with the size of the ostrich. An ostrich egg is only about 2 percent of the weight of the female. Ostriches often lay their eggs in a group nest with one **dominant** female, called the "major hen," and some other females, called "minor hens." The major hen can lay as many as 10 eggs in the nest, while the minor hens will lay only a few eggs. Both the major hen and the male sit on the eggs.

A male Common Ostrich beside his nest.

This kiwi skeleton with an egg shows you just how big the egg is compared to the bird. The egg is close to 20 percent of the female's body weight.

**3** The North Island Brown Kiwi lays the biggest egg compared with its body size. Kiwi eggs are close to 20 percent of the female's body weight. Most of the time, kiwis lay only one egg in their clutch, but occasionally they will lay two. The male kiwi sits on the egg for close to 80 days before it hatches. (The female leaves the nest but stays nearby.) He only leaves the egg for short periods so he can find food. The newly hatched young are very advanced and can leave the nest within two to three weeks, though often the whole family will stay together for several months.

An adult North Island Brown Kiwi.

A nesting Canada Goose.

**4** The Canada Goose nests throughout much of North America. **Subspecies** of Canada Goose can vary in size, and egg size also differs depending on the subspecies. A Canada Goose normally lays an egg every 36 hours, and the weight of the egg is about 4 percent of the female's body weight. Only the female sits on the egg, but the male usually stays close to the nest and helps defend the eggs and young from predators. The young are active after they hatch and will leave the nest in about one or two days.

**5** The Domestic Chicken is the most common bird in the world today, with an estimated population of over 20 billion. It was **domesticated** from the Red Junglefowl of southeast Asia more than 8,000 years ago. Males are known as roosters and females are known as hens. Today, commercial hens lay about 300 eggs a year. They also lay different colors of eggs: blue, green, brown or white, depending on the breed. As hens get older they lay larger eggs but not as many.

A Domestic Chicken.

A pair of American Robins with their chicks.

A Ruby-throated Hummingbird.

6. American Robins also breed throughout much of North America. Unlike the Canada Goose, robins do not vary much in size, and their eggs are all about the same size as well. A robin egg weighs about 8 percent of the female that laid it. That may not sound like much, but don't forget that robins usually lay four or five eggs in their nest over four or five days. That works out to around 40 percent of their body weight. Robin chicks are born almost naked and blind. They will stay in the nest for close to two weeks before they **fledge**.

7. Hummingbirds lay the smallest eggs of all birds. A Ruby-throated Hummingbird's egg looks like a small, white jellybean and is just over 1 centimeter (0.4 inches) long. However, compared with the female hummingbird, one egg is big — nearly 17 percent of the weight of a mature Ruby-throated Hummingbird! The female will lay one to three eggs and sit on them for 12 or 13 days. She looks after the young herself with no help from the male. The young will stay in the nest for almost two weeks before they fledge.

# How Big Is That Egg?

**Want to understand how big a particular egg is? Next time you're at the grocery store, check out the fruit!**

A hummingbird egg is about the size of a raisin.

A robin egg is about the size of a grape.

An ostrich egg is about the size of a large grapefruit.

A chicken egg is about the size of a kiwifruit.

An Elephant Bird egg was about the size of a watermelon.

# CHAPTER 3
# SHAPE

Bird eggs come in many different shapes, though most have a bigger end and a narrower end. New research has found that egg shape is related to flying ability. Birds that spend lots of time in the air and are good flyers require lightweight bodies that glide smoothly through the air. This means their eggs will be longer and more pointed. Birds that don't need to fly as much will have rounder, more spherical eggs. Other research shows that nesting sites and the position the birds use to sit on their eggs may also affect the shape of the eggs. There are likely other reasons why egg shape varies that are related to the parents' body shape and how many eggs are laid. Interestingly, the shape of the egg is determined by the membrane that wraps around the yolk and albumen, before the eggshell is even added.

Four basic bird egg shapes: (clockwise from top left) round, oval, sub-elliptical and pyriform.

# ROUND

Owl eggs are not completely spherical, but they are rounder than most bird eggs. Many owl species have elliptical (almost-round) eggs, and it doesn't seem to matter where they nest. Great Horned Owls sometimes lay their eggs on an abandoned stick nest, in cavities and occasionally on the ground. Owls usually stand upright when they are resting, but when they are incubating their eggs they sit just like other birds.

# OVAL

Black-bellied Plovers are members of the shorebird family. They are strong flyers and breed in the Arctic. They almost always lay four big eggs. The weight of each one is about 16 percent of the female plover's weight. The eggs are oval, and the pointed ends are always positioned inward so the incubating parent can cover all the eggs and keep them warm.

# PYRIFORM

Common Murres are strong-flying **seabirds** that nest on cliffs. They have the most pointed eggs of all birds — what are called pyriform, or pear-shaped, eggs. Scientists once thought pyriform eggs would roll in a tight circle so that they couldn't fall off the cliffs. Now it turns out that the pointed egg shape may stop the eggs from rolling in the first place. It may also help the eggs stay cleaner and let more oxygen get to the embryo. Murres stand more upright when they incubate their eggs, so the shape may also help keep the eggs warmer.

# SUB-ELLIPTICAL

Like murres, Double-crested Cormorants are also strong-flying seabirds, but instead of nesting on cliffs they nest on flat stick nests in trees or on the ground. Cormorants lay sub-elliptical eggs, which look a little like someone stretched a chicken egg in the middle. Like those of most birds, cormorant eggs lie horizontally during incubation, but they do not have to be arranged in any specific way.

# CHAPTER 4
# COLOR

One of the most beautiful things about bird eggs is the wonderful variety of colors and patterns. Each egg is like a little jewel, telling a different evolutionary story. Although groups of birds — like ducks, owls, sparrows and warblers — usually have similar egg colors, patterns and sizes, each species' egg is unique. Even individual females lay slightly different-colored eggs from the others in the clutch. No egg is exactly the same.

For many species, the egg's color and pattern may be related to where the bird nests. Birds that nest in dark places (like cavities) often have white eggs. Birds that nest on the ground often have **camouflaged** eggs. But there are always exceptions to the rule. In some cases, researchers don't know why eggs have certain colors and patterns. Of course, it doesn't make the eggs any less beautiful.

45

Herring Gulls lay two or three light brown eggs with a few dark spots scattered around each one. The eggs would be obvious on a white background, but they are more camouflaged in the gull's grassy nest.

The American Kestrel is the smallest member of the North American falcon family. Their eggs have a similar color and pattern as other falcon eggs. Other falcons lay their eggs in abandoned stick nests in trees or on dirt or gravel on cliffs or building ledges, but kestrels nest in cavities. Birds that nest in dark cavities usually have white eggs, so the color of the American Kestrel's eggs would suggest that their ancestor might have nested in more open sites in the past.

Willow Ptarmigans are masters of camouflage. In the winter, their feathers are white, but in the summer the females **molt** and replace their white feathers with **mottled**, brown ones to blend in with the ground and plants. Ptarmigan eggs are just as interesting. They have a light brown base but are heavily mottled with dark brown spots and blotches. The mottling helps break up the outline of the egg, making it harder to notice it against a background.

48

Sandhill Cranes begin laying their eggs in late winter or spring, before plants have begun to turn green. They like to nest in **wetlands** with lots of plants that are light brown. Their eggs are also light brown, with some slightly darker blotching. It may not look like it from the photo, but the eggs are well hidden in the background.

Common Murres breed in large, dense colonies on sea cliffs. Their eggs come in many different colors and patterns. Research has shown that murres can identify their own eggs, which is a big help in a crowded colony. Also, individual females produce similar-looking eggs year after year.

The Gray Catbird got its name from the meowing calls it makes as it looks for food in dense bushes and shrubs. These are the same places where catbirds build their nests. The eggs are a pretty, dark greenish-blue color. Blue eggs are not well camouflaged, but they may be important for catbirds for other reasons. Studies have shown that catbirds can recognize their own egg color and will throw out the white, spotted eggs of brood parasites, like the Brown-headed Cowbird.

The Great-crested Flycatcher is another cavity-nesting species that doesn't follow the "white egg" rule. They don't like to have their nest too deep in a cavity, so seeing their eggs may not be a big problem. Their eggs have a light, yellowish-brown base finished off with beautiful reddish-brown streaking. Great-crested Flycatchers also have the interesting habit of lining their nests with discarded snake skins and plastics.

Warblers are a large group of birds in North America, with over 50 species. Most lay light-colored eggs with some brown spots. The spots are concentrated near the bigger end and appear in the shape of a wreath or crown. Warbler eggs can be difficult to tell apart unless you know a little about the nest as well. For example, Yellow Warblers, like the one shown here, usually nest low down in bushes and are common hosts of eggs from the Brown-headed Cowbird. Can you spot the cowbird egg in this photo?

Red-winged Blackbird eggs have a light blue base and are scribbled, marbled and spotted with brownish-black marks. The marks are often near the bigger end of the egg.

A Northern Mockingbird lays pale green eggs with light brown spots overlaid with darker brown spots. The spots are more concentrated near the bigger end of the egg, like a crown. Despite all the colors, the eggs seem well camouflaged in the vegetation, though this nest with all the plastic does stand out a bit.

Rose-breasted Grosbeaks nest in forests. Like the mockingbird, they lay greenish-blue eggs, but the brown spots are wreathed around the egg rather than concentrated at the top. Male and female grosbeaks will sometimes sing from their nests, which seems like a strange way to hide where your eggs are.

# Spot the Egg!

Some eggs blend so well into their backgrounds, they're very hard to see. Check out this gallery of photos and see if you can spot the eggs in each image. And don't forget to watch where you're stepping! For the answers, turn to page 80.

# CHAPTER 5
# LOCATION

Birds need a safe place to lay their eggs. They need to be able to keep their eggs warm and protect them from predators. When we think of a bird nest, we usually picture it in a tree or a bush. Lots of birds nest in trees, but they can also nest in many other places. Some birds nest on the ground, and some even nest underground. Others nest on cliffs, in caves or on human-made structures. And birds that live in wetlands and by lakes often nest on or near the water.

## TREE NESTING

Nesting in a tree or bush is a great place to raise a family. Trees offer places to hide your eggs from the curious eyes of predators, and leaves and branches give additional protection for the parents and young during bad weather. Birds that nest in **evergreen trees** can start nesting earlier in the year. Birds that nest in **deciduous trees** and shrubs usually wait until the leaves grow back in the spring. The best time to look for old bird nests in trees is in the winter, when the leaves have fallen from the trees and bushes.

An osprey lands on its stick nest atop a snag, which is a standing dead tree.

Eastern Kingbirds usually nest in trees and shrubs in a variety of habitats. Sometimes the nests are out in the open, but other times they are well hidden and protected. Kingbird nests are shaped like a cup. They are messy but sturdy and are made of grasses and sticks. They are often lined with plant fibers, animal hair and fine grasses. Kingbird eggs have an off-white base color with striking reddish-brown spots near the bigger end. The number and size of spots varies among females but are consistent for each bird's clutch. Kingbirds, like many species, will sometimes include pieces of plastic in their nests. No one is really sure why — maybe it is for decoration!

Common Ravens are found in North America, Europe and Asia. They are one of the world's most intelligent bird species. Ravens often build their nests in trees but will also use cliff faces, old barns, bridges and other human-made structures. The nest is shaped like a big, bulky cup and is well lined with animal hair and plant material. Ravens begin nesting early in the year, so a warm lining is important for their mottled, greenish-blue eggs and their young.

The Red-eyed Vireo builds a hanging nest suspended between two twigs on a small tree branch. The nests are usually made with bark strips and grasses bound together with plant fibers and spiderwebs. They are lined with pine needles, fine grasses and animal hair. The female builds the nest by herself and lays three or four pretty, white eggs with brown spots near the bigger end.

## CAVITY NESTING

Many birds nest in holes or cavities in trees. Tree cavities are ideal places to nest because they offer protection from weather and predators. Some birds, like woodpeckers and chickadees, dig their own holes. Other birds, like owls and wrens, will use natural cavities like knotholes or broken branches. There is a third group of birds, like some ducks and swallows, that will use holes that woodpeckers have already made.

Northern Flickers, a type of woodpecker, will either reuse a nest or dig a new one in the spring. Females and males both help make a new nest, and they almost always choose a tree that is already dead or diseased. It will take the pair about two weeks to dig out the cavity. When the female is ready to lay her eggs, she will lay them directly on the wood chips she made while digging out the cavity. Flickers usually lay six to nine glossy, white eggs, which take about 12 days to hatch. After the flickers finish nesting, other birds and animals may use the cavity in later years.

Eastern Bluebirds also use nest cavities to keep their eggs safe, but their nests look much different from a flicker's wood-chip nest. Although they use existing holes or cavities (in fact, they might use an old flicker nest), bluebirds build a complete nest inside the cavity. Today they often use nest boxes made by people trying to help bluebirds. Once the parents have chosen the nest cavity, the female starts to add nesting material. It usually takes about a week for her to build a cup-shaped nest with dry grasses and fine twigs. She will often lay four to six pale blue eggs and will keep them warm by herself. The eggs hatch in about 14 days, and both parents feed the young.

## GROUND NESTING

Laying your eggs on the ground means you can nest in lots of different habitats, but it does come with some risks. There are more predators on the ground, and if you choose the wrong place your eggs might be stepped on accidentally. Many birds nest in tall grasses, beside fallen logs or under bushes to help hide their eggs, but other birds nest out in the open and rely on different strategies to keep their eggs safe.

Killdeer often nest in open areas like parking lots or on the edges of gravel roads. They will even nest on flat gravel rooftops occasionally. Their nest is not much more than a shallow scrape in the ground. Both the male and female use their breasts and feet to make the shallow nest. They then decorate it with pieces of light-colored vegetation, rocks and/or shells. Killdeer lay four buff-colored, blotched eggs — four being the perfect number to fit under them snugly. Interestingly, Killdeer young are almost the same color as the eggs they emerge from. If a predator approaches the nest, the adults will often leave the eggs and try to distract the predator to lure them away.

Common Nighthawks also lay their eggs on the ground and will use gravel rooftops in urban areas, just like Killdeer. Nighthawks don't build a nest, though females will often use the same location for several years. Female nighthawks lay two eggs and will sit on them for 18 days before they hatch. They will only leave the eggs in the evening for a quick snack before returning to the nest. Their eggs are creamy to pale olive in color and heavily speckled with gray, brown and black. Nighthawks rely on camouflage to protect their eggs. They will also try to distract predators or even hiss to scare them away.

## UNDERGROUND NESTING

It may sound crazy, but laying your eggs underground might be the safest place of all. The nest is probably a little dark inside, but the eggs are safe from most predators, and you don't have to worry too much about the wind, rain or cold. Like those of most cavity nesters, the eggs of underground nesters are generally white, which makes them easier for the parent to see. Some species will nest in long burrows they dig themselves. Others, like the Burrowing Owl, will nest in old ground squirrel tunnels. Some birds use human-made structures, like tunnels, culverts and drainpipes. Other birds will simply nest in a crevice or under a rock.

Atlantic Puffins spend most of their time at sea and only come to land to build their nests, lay their eggs and raise their young. Every year, the female lays a single white egg in a shallow burrow near the top of a sea cliff. Nesting locations can be hard to find, so puffins mostly nest in dense colonies, often near other cliff-nesting seabirds. Nests sites are typically reused for several years. Do you think puffins like sitting on their eggs in a warm, cozy burrow, away from the wind and water?

In the Arctic even summer can be cold and windy. There are no trees, so most birds nest on the ground. The Northern Wheatear, a small songbird, goes underground to nest. They lay their eggs under rocks or in rocky crevices, well protected from the cold. They build a grassy nest lined with warm feathers and plant fibers, where they will lay five to seven light blue eggs.

## NESTING ON WATER

There are many bird species that spend most of their lives on or near water. Some live on the ocean, some on lakes and rivers and some in wetlands. Building a nest and laying eggs near water can be difficult, but different species have found inventive ways to overcome the challenges.

Common Loons are excellent swimmers and strong flyers, but they are very bad walkers. Their legs and feet are positioned so far back on their bodies that it is difficult for them to walk very far. As a result, loons always build their nests and lay one or two brown, splotchy eggs close to water. They like to nest on the shores of islands. They will also make their own "nest island" by gathering nearby vegetation until they have built a little mound above the water that is safe and dry. Loons have to choose the site carefully so waves from boats and strong winds do not cover their eggs with water.

Pied-billed Grebes nest on the water in marshes and other wetlands. They build a floating platform of dead plant material that is anchored to nearby vegetation and well hidden from view. Grebe nests and eggs are often wet, but this does not seem to affect nesting success. Parents will even cover and hide their clutch of five to eight eggs with wet nesting material if they leave to feed. The eggs are a shiny pale blue when they are first laid, but they quickly become dirty and stained from the wet vegetation.

## NESTING ON HUMAN-MADE STRUCTURES

Although most birds nest and lay their eggs in natural environments, there are many species that use human-made structures. Human environments can provide a variety of excellent nesting locations that are similar to natural sites and often more plentiful in urban and rural areas. Some of our most common and numerous birds, like the American Robin, European Starling, Mourning Dove, Red-winged Blackbird and Canada Goose, now live near or in our barns, villages, towns and cities. Finding food, avoiding predators and protecting yourself from the weather is sometimes easier when you have a literal roof over your head.

The Barn Swallow once commonly nested on cliffs or banks along rivers. Today they are more frequently found in or on buildings, on light fixtures and under bridges and in culverts. They build their nests by collecting mouthfuls of mud and then sticking them together. The nest is often built on a vertical surface, usually close to a horizontal ceiling, so their three to seven white eggs are well protected. The nests are lined with feathers, some grasses and other plant materials.

Chimney Swifts are small, fast-flying acrobatic birds that catch all their food in flight. They fly all day long, only coming to **roost** in the evening or when they are nesting. Can you guess where Chimneys Swifts like to nest? Here's a hint: it's in their name. Chimney Swifts love to nest inside chimneys, but they've also been found nesting in barns, old buildings and even lighthouses. Before using human-made structures, they nested in hollow trees and caves. They lay their four or five white eggs in a nest constructed with small twigs that they glue together on a vertical surface with their saliva.

The Red-tailed Hawk is one of the most common **birds of prey** in North America. They like to nest up high so they can get a good view of the habitat around them. They typically nest in trees, but recently they have started moving into cities and using human-made structures. Today, it is not unusual to see hawk nests on hydro towers, streetlights, lampposts and even window ledges high up on buildings. Red-tails usually lay two to four splotched or speckled eggs. Their nests are large, so the young hawks have lots of room to grow and move around.

# That's a Weird Place for a Nest!

Ever find a bird nest that felt a bit out of place? Check out these unusual nesting spots!

This American Robin built its nest on a traffic light.

Looking for privacy, this House Finch laid its eggs in a women's washroom.

This Carolina Wren made a paper towel dispenser its temporary home.

This Black-throated Green Warbler decided to keep its eggs cozy in a section of curling birch bark.

# CHAPTER 6
# CONSERVATION AND PROTECTION

The breeding season is one of the most important times in a bird's life. This is when birds will lay their eggs and raise their families. It is also one of the most sensitive times for birds, and we need to be extra careful not to cause them any harm. In North America most birds breed in spring and early summer, when the weather is warmer and there is plenty of food. The breeding season is short though, and birds only have a few months to find a mate, build their nests, lay their eggs and raise their families. If a predator finds their nest or if the nest is disturbed too much, the parents might not be able to breed again until the following year.

Here are a couple of things you can do to help breeding birds and their eggs.

## MONITORING NESTS

We have learned a lot about birds by observing their behavior during the breeding season, but there is still so much more to learn. And

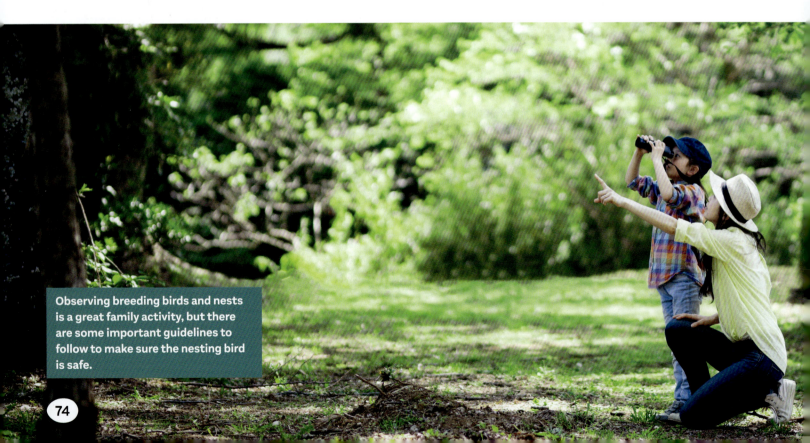

Observing breeding birds and nests is a great family activity, but there are some important guidelines to follow to make sure the nesting bird is safe.

we can all help. Scientists lead the research, but any person who loves birds can also contribute to bird knowledge by becoming a citizen/community scientist and monitoring breeding bird populations.

You don't have to travel far to help. You can record observations from your backyard, your local park or anytime you are out for a walk in the country or city.

For instance, if you're out for a spring walk near your home and you happen to see a robin with a beak full of grass, there is a good chance it is building a nest. If you see a robin with a mouth full of worms, it might be feeding its young in a nest nearby. If you have time, the best thing to do is just watch the bird and see what happens next. Within a couple of minutes, the bird will probably fly to its nest and continue to build it or feed its young. Now that you know where the nest is, you must be extra careful not to cause too much disturbance nearby.

If you decide you want to regularly monitor what is happening at the nest, be very careful and follow these guidelines:

- If you are watching a nest, always make sure you are not on someone else's private property.
- Observe from a distance at first and don't get too close. You don't want to disturb the bird or attract the attention of predators. Using binoculars will allow you to observe nesting activity without disturbing the birds.
- Don't spend too much time close to the nest.

**Here are some general rules that will help you be a successful observer:**

- **Always approach a nesting area with care and caution.**
- **Be aware of the bird's behavior. If it looks nervous and you are close to the nest, move farther away and watch from a distance.**
- **Look out for any potential nest predators so you don't unintentionally show them where the bird is nesting.**

- Minimize disturbance at the nest site. Observe quietly and try not to break any branches or step on plants.
- Every time you visit the nest, try approaching it from a different route so predators are not following your trail.
- Don't go to the nest every day. Once or twice a week will still provide great information about what is happening.
- Don't handle the eggs or young. If the nest is in a tree or bush, you can use a mirror on a stick (inspection mirror) to see how many eggs are in the nest when the parent goes off to feed.

And always remember that the safety of the bird comes first. If you think you might be disturbing a nest, please be extra cautious. The bird's safety is more important than collecting data about the nest.

Black-capped Chickadees are great starter birds to observe as they are easily attracted by bird feeders as well as nest boxes.

## GETTING INVOLVED

If you are interested in observing breeding birds, there many organized programs you can get involved with. Here are just a few:

**Project Nestwatch — birdscanada.org/bird-science/project-nestwatch**
Project NestWatch is a monitoring program for breeding birds and nesting activity in Canada. Scientists and citizen scientists can submit nest observations to help forward research and the conservation of birds and their natural habitats.

**NestWatch — nestwatch.org**
NestWatch, run by the Cornell Lab of Ornithology, is an America-wide nest-monitoring program where citizen scientists can record data about nests. The data helps researchers understand the current condition of breeding bird populations and how they might be changing with climate change and habitat degradation.

**Breeding Bird Atlases — birdscanada.org/bird-science/breeding-bird-atlases**
With support from volunteer citizen scientists in Canada, Breeding Bird Atlases is a program that maps and records the distribution and relative abundance of birds in a given province during a five-year period.

**Canadian Lakes Loon Survey — birdscanada.org/bird-science/canadian-lakes-loon-survey**
Citizen scientists can help track the breeding success of Common Loons by monitoring loon territories, chick hatching and fledgling survival over the summer.

**eBird — ebird.org/about**
This online platform for birders, bird scientists and the public allows users to document and share their bird observations. The Canadian eBird platform can be found at **ebird.org/canada/home**.

**iNaturalist — inaturalist.org**
iNaturalist is a citizen science platform where users can record, share and discuss observations of the natural world. By doing so, they are adding to biodiversity research. Users can document and identify plants, animals, mushrooms and other organisms on this site. The Canadian iNaturalist platform can be found at **inaturalist.ca**.

## BUILDING NEST BOXES

You can also help breeding birds by building nest boxes. This can be a lot of fun, and it may help the birds in your neighborhood. You can build boxes for ducks, owls, bluebirds, swallows and even wrens. You can also buy nest boxes at many nature stores.

You will need to do a little research on the best nest box for a particular species. Each bird species requires specific habitat needs and nest sites, and certain birds like a particular hole size for their box.

Before installing a nest box, make sure you have permission from the people who own the land where you want to put it.

To learn more, check out this website: nestwatch.org/learn/all-about-birdhouses

A Tree Swallow using a nest box.

# GLOSSARY

**Altricial:** This describes a chick that is born blind and helpless and needs lots of care from its parent(s) before it can take care of itself. See *Precocial*.

**Birds of prey:** Bird species that hunt and feed on smaller animals. They often have hooked bills, sharp claws and good eyesight. Examples include owls, hawks and eagles.

**Camouflage:** When birds or eggs blend in with their surroundings so they are not easily seen by predators. For example, some eggs are a similar color or pattern as the places that they're laid on, which makes it hard for a predator to find and eat them.

**Cavity:** A chamber that a bird makes or finds in a tree or stump.

**Colony:** A large group of birds, all of the same species, that nest close to each other.

**Deciduous tree:** A tree or shrub that sheds its leaves yearly, usually in fall.

**Domesticate:** To tame an animal to keep as a pet or on a farm.

**Dominant:** Some animals live in groups in which one or two individuals rank higher than the rest. These individuals are considered the dominant members of the group. They may have their pick of food and mates and may also be responsible for defending their territory.

**Ecology:** The area of science that studies how species interact with each other and their environments.

**Embryo:** An unborn or unhatched offspring that is developing. For birds, this is the unhatched chick that is developing inside an egg.

**Evergreen tree:** A tree or shrub that keeps its leaves all year round.

**Fertilize:** In animals, this means to make a new animal life by joining a female egg cell with a male cell.

**Fledge:** When a young bird is first able to fly. It may also be used to describe when a young bird leaves the nest.

**Invertebrate:** Animals that don't have a backbone, such as spiders, worms, snails, crabs and insects.

**Molt:** When a bird sheds its old feathers to make way for new feathers.

**Mottled:** When something is marked with spots, streaks and/or patches of different colors.

**Ovary:** A female reproductive organ where egg cells are made and stored.

**Pigment (eggs):** A substance made by the female bird's shell gland that produces different colors and patterns on eggs.

**Porous:** Having tiny holes through which liquid or air can pass.

**Precocial:** This describes a chick that is born with open eyes and downy feathers and can feed itself and move around shortly after hatching. See *Altricial*.

**Predator:** An animal that kills and eats other animals.

**Reproduction:** The creation of offspring.

**Roost:** To settle for rest or sleep.

**Seabird:** A bird that is adapted to live on the coast and open ocean. Examples include murres and gulls.

**Shorebird:** A special type of bird that is often found near shorelines or wet areas. Examples include sandpipers, plovers, avocets and phalaropes.

**Songbird:** A bird with specialized feet that can grasp branches and a vocal organ called a syrinx (specifically from a group of birds known as the Passeri). Examples include thrushes, warblers, ravens and sparrows. Songbirds have the most species found in any bird family.

**Species:** Animals that share common characteristics and can successfully reproduce with each other.

**Subspecies:** Certain groups within a species may live in a specific area and as a result vary in size, shape or some other physical characteristic. These subspecies can still successfully mate with other individuals within their species. See *Species*.

**Vertebrate:** Animals that have a backbone, or spinal column, such as birds, mammals, fish and reptiles.

**Waterfowl:** Any bird that spends most of its time on or near water. Examples include ducks, geese and swans.

**Wetland:** An ecosystem that is flooded with water either permanently or for long periods of time. Examples include swamps, marshes and bogs.

# INDEX

Page numbers in *italics* represent charts and photos.

about eggs, 6–33
albumen, 7, *7*, 40
altricial, 78
American Golden-Plovers, 31, *31*
American Kestrels, 47, *47*
American Redstarts, 22, *22*
American Robins, *23*, 38, *38*
American White Pelicans, *23*
Atlantic Puffins, 10, *10*, *23*, 66, *66*

Bald Eagles, 14, *14*, *23*
Barn Swallows, 70, *70*
binoculars, 75
birds of prey, 72
Black-bellied Plovers, 42, *42*
Black-billed Cuckoos, *26*
blackbirds, 54, *54*
Black-capped Chickadees, *23*, 76, *76*
Black-legged Kittiwakes, 30, *30*
Blue Jays, *23*
bluebirds, 63, *63*
breeding seasons, 74
brood parasitism, 24–7, 51
brood patch, 16
Brown-headed Cowbirds, 27, *27*
Burrowing Owls, 66

calcium carbonate, 7–8
camouflage, 45–6, *46*, 48, 65
Canada Geese, 33, *33*, 37, *37*
cavities, 25, 30, 41, 45, 47, 52, 62–3
cells, 6–7, *7*
chickadees, *23*, 76, *76*
chickens, 37, *37*, 39
chicks, 34, 78
Chimney Swifts, 71, *71*
clutch size, 10–15
collecting eggs, 5
colonies, 10
color of eggs, 37, 45–57, 69
Common Loons, *23*, 68, *68*
Common Murres, 43, *43*, 50, *50*
Common Nighthawks, 65, *65*
Common Ravens, *23*, 60, *60*
conservation and protection, 74–7
cowbirds, 24, 27, *27*
cranes, 49, *49*
cuckoos, 24, 26, *26*

deciduous trees, 58
dinosaurs, 5
dissolving eggshells, 8
Domestic Chickens, 37, *37*
domestication, 37
dominant, 34
Double-crested Cormorants, 44, *44*
doves, 12, *12*
ducks, 11, *11*, 25, *25*
dumping eggs, 25

eagles, 14, *14*, *23*
Eastern Bluebirds, 63, *63*
Eastern Kingbirds, 59, *59*
eating eggs, 28
ecology, 5
egg predators. *See* predators
eggshells, 7–8, *7–8*, 31, 34
Elephant Birds, 34, *34*, 39
embryos, 7, 43
Emperor Penguins, *23*
evergreen trees, 58

falcons, 47, *47*
fertilization, 7, 9
fledge, 38
flying, 40

glossary, 78
Golden-crowned Kinglets, 14, *23*
Gray Catbirds, 51, *51*
Great Blue Herons, *23*
Great Horned Owls, 41, *41*
Great-crested Flycatchers, 52, *52*
ground nesting, 64–5

hawks, 72, *72*
herons, *23*
Herring Gulls, 45, *46*
human-made structures nesting, 70–3
hummingbirds, *23*, 38, *38*, 39

incubation of eggs, 16–23, *23*, 38, 63, 65
invertebrates, 5

Killdeers, 64, *64*

laying eggs, 9
location of eggs, 58–73
loons, *23*, 68, *68*

major/minor hens, 34
making eggs, 7, *7*
membranes, 7, *7*, 40
molt, 48
monitoring nests, 74–5
Morning Doves, 12, *12*
mottled, 48, 60
Mute Swans, *23*

nesting. *See* cavities; incubation of eggs; location of eggs; timing of eggs
nesting boxes, 25, 63, 77, *77*
nighthawks, 65, *65*
North Island Brown Kiwis, *23*, 36, *36*
Northern Flickers, 62, *62*
Northern Mockingbirds, 55, *55*
Northern Pintail ducks, 11, *11*
Northern Wheatear, 67, *67*
number of eggs, 10–15

observing, 74–5
oology, 5
organized programs, 76
ospreys, *58*
ostriches, *23*, 34, *34*, 39
ova, 6–7, *7*
ovary, 7, *7*
Ovenbirds, 29
oviduct, 7, *7*
oviparous and ovoviviparous animals, 6
owls, 21, *21*, *23*, 41, *41*, 66

pelicans, *23*
penguins, *23*
Pied-billed Grebes, 69
pigeons, 20, *20*
pigments, 7
Pileated Woodpeckers, *23*, 30
plovers, 31–2, *31–2*, 42, *42*
porousness, 7
precocial, 78
predators, 5, 28, 28–33, 64, 65, 74, 75
puffins, 10, *10*, 66, *66*

ravens, *23*, 60, *60*
Red-eyed Vireos, 61, *61*
Red-necked Phalaropes, 19, *19*
Red-tailed Hawks, 72, *72*
Red-winged Blackbirds, 54, *54*
reproduction, 5
robins, *23*, 38, *38*, 39
Rock Pigeons, 20, *20*
rolling eggs, 43
roosts, 71
Rose-breasted Grosbeaks, 56, *56*
Ruby-throated Hummingbirds, *23*, 38, *38*

Sandhill Cranes, 49, *49*
seabirds, *23*, 30, *30*, 43–4, *43–4*, 46, *46*, 50, *50*. *See also* puffins
Semipalmated Plovers, 32, *32*
shape of eggs, 40–4, *40*
Sharp-tailed Grouse, 18, *18*
shorebirds, 13, *13*, 42
Short-eared Owls, 21, *21*
size of eggs, 34–9, *34*, *39*, 42
Snowy Albatross, *23*
Snowy Owls, *23*
Song Sparrows, 14, *14*
songbirds, 14–15, *14–15*, *23*, 67, *67*
species, 9
spot the egg, 57
subspecies, 37
swallows, 70, *70*
swans, 11, *23*

timing of eggs, 16–23, *23*, 37
touching eggs, 75
Tundra Swans, 11

underground nesting, 66–7

vertebrates, 5
viviparous animals, 6

warblers, 22, *22*, 53, *53*
water nesting, 68–9
waterfowl, 11, 24
wetlands, 49
Whimbrels, 13, *13*
Willow Ptarmigans, 48, *48*
Wood Ducks, 25, *25*
woodpeckers, *23*, 30, 62, *62*

Yellow Warblers, 53, *53*
Yellow-billed Cuckoos, 26
yolks, 7, *7*, 40

# ACKNOWLEDGMENTS

First and foremost, I would like to express my great thanks and appreciation to my editor, Julie Takasaki, for her knowledge and considerable assistance with this book. I would also like to thank the Royal Ontario Museum staff, Paul Eekhoff, Senior Photographer, and Nicola Woods, Rights and Reproduction Coordinator, for their help with the images. And thanks to my father, George K. Peck, and my family, Emily, Sydney and Georgia, for their support in allowing me to do what I love to do.

## PHOTO CREDITS

All photos © 2024 Mark Peck, except as listed below:

imageBROKER/S & D & K Maslowski/Alamy Stock Photo: 71.

James M. Richards: 26 (inset).

Julie Takasaki: 8.

*Quaternary of Madagascar* by Monnier, 1913 (public domain): 34 (top).

North Island Brown Kiwi, Apteryx mantelli, collected 26 August 1940, Rotorua, New Zealand. CC BY 4.0. Te Papa (OR.016582): 36 (top).

Randy Mehoves/Alamy Stock Photo: 16.

Courtesy of ROM (Royal Ontario Museum), Toronto, Canada. Photo by Paul Eekhoff © ROM: 35, 40, 50 (main photo).

**Shutterstock**
Aggie 11: 20 (inset).
akepong srichaichana: 39.
Angelo Spillo: 70 (main photo).
bergamont: 39.
David Keep: 6 (bottom middle).
Eva Lorenz: 6 (bottom right).
Hakase_420: 74–75.
happykamill: 6 (top).
Kate Cuzko: 39.
Maks Narodenko: 39.
Mark Schocken: 9.
PixaHub: 39.
Redfox1980: 73 (top left).
Reesor Photography: 23 (bottom).
Roberto Dani: 36 (bottom).
Roger de la Harpe: 34 (bottom).
rontav: 3.
Sandra Standbridge: 28 (bottom).
Steve Bower: 58.
Vishnevskiy Vasily: 45, 60 (main).
yhelfman: 28 (top).
yvontrep: 38 (left).

## Spot the Egg! Answer Key
(photo puzzle on page 57)